And in a truly autistic social moment, this stranger said "Quadrant means four. You don't live in Portland." Only in Portland's infinite quirkiness would there be five quadrants and I would be the one portrayed as dumb. I feel like those are the only types of interactions that I have. I know about something obscure before other people so my knowledge threatens their self-image and nobody wants to acknowledge the possibility that it is real. So they try to paint me as ignorant, because I have fewer social skills than they do.

I burned out into the sidewalk, right there. I wanted to just quit everything and melt onto a mattress on the sidewalk in the hot sun. I'm sure these people whom I had just met meant this as a moment of pleasant small talk, but I couldn't speak again for the rest of the day. This turned into a major event in my trip, though I'm sure no one else involved even remembers it 22 years later. It was only the next morning when a different stranger came up and said "I've been to North Portland. I know what you're talking about" that I felt like a person again and resumed interactions. Without that, I'm not sure how I would have managed myself for the rest of that trip.

This story isn't unique. Though it's rare that I recovered from it quickly. Things like this happen to us *all the time*. And the results often linger for weeks or even years. There's a power in sharing these stories, of how we moved past burnout, and how it sometimes ruins dreams. Many things that we set out to accomplish in life prove impossible due to burnout, so it's a matter of setting the pace and putting the safeguards in place.

I frequently find myself in the position of talking to a stranger, who will charge up a thorny hill with statements like "Well, it's not like a neurodivergent person can't go to college..." and the answer to that is "Well, I guess we *can* but with tremendous difficulty and much less likelihood of success." The reasons for this are similar to the reasons that everything is different for autistic and neurodiverse people: the world isn't built with us in mind. It can be difficult or feel shameful to admit that we have no idea how to do something that most people do everyday without instruction or thinking about it. That's the very definition of privilege. And the sooner that everyone keeps that in the back of their mind, the sooner that we can function more equitably.

One final note is that we made the difficult decision to change the title of this series. After five years of battling for a neurodivergent rights movement, we found that the world had shifted from the punk rock universe of GB Jones and Bruce LaBruce's 1985 "Don't Be Gay" manifesto that Eliot and I grew up with. While we still believe that reclamation is the only way to take power back from the people who used slurs and harmful words to us, most conversations with potential contributors were instead spent on the nuances between "neurodiverse" and "neurodivergent" or how each contributor would then be responsible to justify how our use of *Proud to be*

Retarded was being used by people who had suffered for 40 years under that mantle. In the end, we felt that it was distracting from our mission of autistic acceptance and a neurodivergent rights movement. We're still proud and in your face. But after being removed from innumerable therapists' offices and received dozens of "Sorry, I'd love to contribute, but I'm not sure that my fans are ready for that..." we decided that we didn't want to be the middle aged punks telling young people that their generation's music sucks and how they should do things. So we learn, evolve, and move on.

WE DON'T TALK ABOUT BURNOUT

Partly Robot

I don't talk about burnout as much as I could. Part of the reason is that one of my big triggers is feeling misunderstood. If I'm anywhere near meltdown territory, it's best not to risk trying to explain to anyone why I honestly couldn't do anything on my day off.

Now, let me backup a little bit. Usually, the moment I decide not to talk about another mild flareup of burnout is on Monday morning. That's when someone at work tries to make some nice small talk with me about whether I did anything interesting over the weekend. If I say something like, "I was exhausted, so I just rested," they'll respond with something enthusiastic like "that's great."

It isn't great. It really isn't. I spent the whole weekend trying not to fall over the edge into totally a state of being totally unable to function around other people. But no one doing the small talk thing on a Monday morning really wants to hear that. So, I'll lie and say it was all right, because we don't talk about burnout.

I didn't know what autistic burnout was for a long time. Mostly, because I didn't know I was autistic. However, I knew I was constantly misunderstood and that made it harder and harder for me to successfully connect

with people in the way that a predominantly neurotypical world requires.

I can trace back my first major burnout episode to the Spring of 1993. It was my freshman year of college. Because I'd always been really good at writing grammatically coherent sentences and performing well on tests, I had a bit of a scholarship. But, in actual college, I was really lousy at figuring out what it was that the university's graduate teaching assistants were trying to get out of me.

The problem was that, unlike high school, I was suddenly in an environment where being a contributor to class discussions actually mattered. And that was hard. It was so hard, in fact, that I stopped going to classes. The classes that I could get through on test scores alone, I went to. The other classes, I didn't go. I couldn't. My body wouldn't let me go somewhere I might be expected to talk to other people. So, my grades tanked, I lost my scholarships, and freaked out my parents.

Somehow I was able to claw myself to some sort of functioning. I went to community college for a while, which was a much more manageable speed for me. I took a drama class as an elective just to force myself to practice talking to people. I started drawing comics and making zines as a way to try to express the stuff that always came out garbled and confusing when I spoke. I cultivated an artsy persona that excused, even demanded, my perceived excentricities be proudly displayed.

But I wasn't over the burnout. I had accumulated a lot of chronic pains, aches, and inflammation all over my body. Through sheer force of will I pushed myself through to get my bachelors degree, and then stalled out. Accomplishing that one goal had taken everything I had. After I burned out all my reserves just to get a piece of paper, I didn't have a clue what to do with my life. I didn't really do much beyond scraping by for the next couple years.

Life continued to have ups and downs I struggled through. It wasn't until at least ten years later that I started to learn about autism. I learned how it described what I'd been experiencing my whole life. I was also finally able to recognize the cycles of meltdowns and burnout and how it affected my physical as well as emotional health. I also finally was able to recognize that not everyone does the amount of work it takes to "function like a normal person" that I have to do.

In the end, I think it's that exhaustion from "functioning like a normal person" that leads to a lot of burnout. Most people really have no idea how draining it is to be the only neurodivergent person in a room full of neurotypicals. Or even a room with one neurotypical. That can be too much.

I've been fortunate to be able to shape my life to fit my strengths. After burning out in my attempt to be an English teacher, I found myself suited to working as classified staff in a school district. The job is tough, but the benefits are good and there's lots of built in time off. Also, I get to interact with kids a lot, which is much easier for me than talking to adults. As a classified paraeducator, I don't have to go to meetings or write lesson plans or figure out classroom management. I just get to work with the coolest kids and share with them some tricks to "functioning like a normal person" without wearing yourself out. If they're ready for them.

But I still get the flare ups of burnout from time to time. Especially when the demands of my employer are so obviously at odds with reality sometimes. Or when I push myself too hard doing social things. Or when I feel myself falling way too far behind on a project that only I care about. Or when it's Monday morning and a coworker acts like it's a good thing I wasn't able to get out of bed at all over the weekend.

I don't like to talk about burnout, because most people have no idea what I'm talking about. Most people don't realize that I have a long list of things I'd rather be getting done on my day off, but I need to take it easy because I can't afford to have another year like 1993. Or 2005. Or 2012, for that matter. All big burnout years that took even more years to recover from.

THE HISTORY OF AUTISM ITSELF

Amelia Nagoski

I had autistic burnout before I co-wrote a book about burnout,[2] or even knew that I was autistic. The best way I've come to understand autistic burnout is the history of autism itself, most widely associated with the research of Nazi-era pediatrician and eugenicist Hans Asperger.

For Asperger, autism stood in opposition to fascism. He, like lots of folks, thought fascism was terrific.[3] The idea is that individuals in a community are like muscle fibers, made stronger by being bound together in uniformity by the fascia. And fascists thought that any individual who wasn't well integrated shouldn't exist.

Indeed, the clinical definition of autism includes difficulty with social/emotional reciprocity. To me, it feels like an inability to be a part of the crowd-unifying ecstatic love of cheering fans of a particular team or band. Hans Asperger despaired of this "deficit," yet he could see how this difference might allow boys to become innovators or leaders in science and engineering—fields highly valued by the Nazis—in service of the greater good.

2 *Burnout: The Secret to Unlocking the Stress Cycle* (Ballantine, 2020, 9781984818324)

3 See *Understanding Eugenics: The U.S. and Nazi Plans to Shape the Gene Pool & Control the Population* (Microcosm, 2021, 9781621062523)

Because we don't connect the same way as non-autistic folks, we also don't take social norms for granted. Which is where Asperger's misogyny becomes clear. He wrote about girls sent to him because they were unruly, having sex, or rejected the necessity of becoming wives and mothers. Girls like me. Asperger sent them to be murdered in the Nazi hospital system.

These are the roots of my diagnosis. For Asperger, autism meant you were unfit to participate in society. The only kids with autistic traits who mattered were boys who could contribute to science. And that remains the stereotype about autism.

A century after autism was first described to modern medicine, burnout became a subject of research. Herbert Freudenberger was hired to help air traffic controllers in the 1970s. Turns out the problem was that their job was stressful, involving life or death decisions with variables beyond their control. Air traffic controllers are doing much better these days because we have computers to handle a lot of the cognition. Because the problem wasn't the people, it was the unmeetable goals and unceasing expectations. The problem was the gap between the people and what was demanded of them.

While workplace burnout remains the most studied burnout, parental burnout and caregiver burnout have also gotten increasing attention. They share the unmeetable goals and unceasing expectations with workplace burnout, as well as an unbridgeable gap between who people are and who they are told they should be.

Autistic burnout is barely studied at all; and, as ever, it is framed within non-autistic perspectives. But when we put together the history of autism with the dynamics of burnout, it's easy to understand why burnout is such a problem for autistic folks.

Everyone faces a gap between who they are and who the world wants them to be. Autism is a difference that reaches across gender, race, physical ability, socio-economic status, and all the other differences that cause friction between individuals and the white-supremacist, cis-hetero-normative, exploitative late capitalist patriarchy. So it always functions to widen an existing gap.

Happily, the cure for that condition is not for us to become more like what the world expects us to be—just as the cure for the air traffic controllers wasn't to work harder, but to create new conditions around them. The cure for us is to create an environment that welcomes and celebrates differences even as fundamental as how we connect with others. The cure for autistic burnout, just like all burnout, is all of us caring for each other.

AT LEAST BE KIND

Eliot K Daughtry

"So, you probably have a résumé that requires a lot of careful crafting to cover the inexplicable times of unemployment. And that résumé might also have some really unpredictable shifts in what your work appears to be. Let me guess, about every five years? Makes it hard to explain a career."

My person Kriss and I were helping clean out a chosen family member's apartment after he died suddenly in 2020. His ex looked at me as if I were a spy, or had some magic crystal ball I consulted. Sitting at his dining room table, she had to be assured that I hadn't seen her papers, that I didn't, in fact, know about her struggles with employment, and that I had never seen her résumé. Nobody had ever identified the obvious on her paper trail, and she reacted like I had stripped her naked. She wasn't ready to be seen for something she viewed as a shameful and secret personal failure, instead of a common neurodivergent reaction to ongoing overload, masking, and being constantly misunderstood.

I would not have been able to identify her struggles if I hadn't learned about patterns that burnout makes over time when one is neurodivergent. It's not the same as the common burnouts that all humans experience, either in how they happen, or how frequently they disrupt our lives. It interferes with sensory processing, triggers conditions that weren't a problem before, and often leads to changes in physical and mental abilities that can become permanently disabling. It often triggers episodes of acute depression, anxiety, and/or PTSD.

The first major burnout I had began before my senior year of high school, the second during my first job out of college, and the third after graduate school while teaching. There were minor ones as well. My life was altered after each one, requiring me to relearn how to be myself, what I can do, and how to interact with others each time. Each burnout left me with altered physical, emotional and intellectual functionality.

By six I knew I was not like most people, but not why. I was both rewarded and punished for my abilities and deficits–huge vocabulary but difficulties with maths. My visual and musical capabilities were never fully understood, but encouraged when convenient, and discouraged when it was too much work for the adults in charge. Between third and fourth grades, nobody could figure out if I was smart or stupid, and I went from special ed to a gifted program in between school systems in the same grade. I didn't really understand what it meant to be a "girl" and I was often labeled a tomboy. My mother was shamed over my lack of femininity and did her best to ignore my nonconformity. My dad encouraged me to make things, regardless of my gender, often remarking on my surprising ability to stay focused on learning difficult things.

The dissonance of puberty, and its socially expected behavior that I understood poorly, threw me into a major depression that enveloped most of my teen years. Comments from teachers on my report cards reflected concerns about my "unmet potential" and reinforced despair, instead of providing encouragement, or a way to find anything positive about myself. When I was removed from the public school gifted program because of poor grades, my mother moved me to an elite private school. That helped some, but created other problems. I wasn't prepared to learn about the social differences, expectations, and behaviors needed in the new environment. Most of it was overwhelming, and I was far from a popular kid.

At first, it was easy for my parents to dismiss what appeared to be an anxiety problem in my senior year. Starting with insomnia, followed by not being able to eat, I was prescribed valium, and sent to weekly psychiatric appointments. It was blamed on my parents' divorce, and diagnosed as separation anxiety, which might have been a kindness from the psychiatrist, who possibly understood that I was struggling with sexuality and gender, without saying anything. There was no discussion of what was going on with my brain function, or what made the anxiety spin up, leading to disabling meltdowns that robbed me of dignity and self control.

The stress manifested my first experiences of dyslexia and dyscalculia as my brain went sideways. Because I was failing my AP classes, I wasn't able to apply to the colleges my parents wanted me to attend. I went to community college instead, which was a good thing. College was far better for me than high school, and community college was a far less competitive and more supportive environment than I expected. My brain started to engage again, and the emotional turmoil started to clear. I came out at eighteen in my first term in college as queer, got involved in the hardcore punk scene, and I put the burnout of my late teens behind me, not wanting to think it had ever happened.

While at community college studying fine art, I met three women that I developed intimate relationships with. The first was a closeted lesbian, the second was not, but there was a significant age difference. The third wasn't openly queer, and was deeply uncomfortable being seen as gay when we became involved. The first two were kind in our breakups, and didn't blame me for shortcomings that ended our relationships. The third wanted something else. She wanted a commitment she did not understand, that I was not prepared to make, and that she could not uphold.

That third girlfriend drove a wedge between me and any friends I had made in college. After I helped her get a scholarship to the School of the Art Institute of Chicago, she threw me out and moved in with my primary mentor, a deep betrayal. I had started working what I considered a dream job at the time–helping document performance art and archiving video recordings of such, and teaching media skills to others. I was blacklisted, blocked from attending a lot of events and treated like a pariah. A friend I made that was on the periphery of the circle of my ex and former mentor let me move in with her, and we became lovers, which should not have happened. Then I came down with mono, and could barely take care of myself for almost three months.

Trying to do anything was overwhelming. Everything became a crisis. My job went from being manageable to working 80 hour weeks in less than six months, and within a year, I was forced to resign. The relationship with my girlfriend became physically and emotionally violent, and was complicated because I also now worked for her. We broke up and I moved into a loft that featured large, drafty windows and abutted the main interstate running through Chicago. It lacked a kitchen and the bathroom was a long way down the hall. Then my ex started stalking me.

A little more than five years after I felt I had recovered from that first burnout, I found myself spiraling into a second, far worse one. Unemployment kept me from starving, but there was barely enough to keep my phone turned on, and not enough to properly heat the loft. Too much time by myself led to constant rumination over my apparent worthlessness, interspersed with a return of an insistent feeling that I was male. Then the unemployment ran out, and I got behind on rent and utilities, and spent weeks sitting in a cold loft with no phone and no power. When I finally called my parents for help, I was given a cold shoulder from both. That fall, Chicago had a bitter cold snap, and I was on the verge of becoming homeless.

Sometimes, one's fate seems doomed, only to have the world offer up sudden salvation. There was a 24 hour diner about a block from the loft, and I often had coffee and a plate of eggs there. I had a dime in my pocket, and intended to ask if I could bus tables or help clean for a meal. The owner was an odd man. He asked me if I knew how to cook short order, which I done while I was in college. The night cook had quit the night before, and now I had a job. Then he heard I needed to move, so he talked to his landlord. I moved into a tiny studio with heat and power included. It was just enough for me to start recovering, get into therapy, and figure out how to start living again.

After I had been working nights at the diner for about a year, a customer asked if I knew anything about computers. When I said yes, he asked me if I would come by his shop to talk when I got off shift. Two weeks later, I became a quality assurance manager for the shop, with a smallish salary and a new career path to explore. I met my future life partner, Kriss, that year at Gay Pride, and we soon moved into a large, dilapidated apartment together.

There were a couple of small problems I had yet to figure out, first: how to address my gender dysphoria, and then how to manage my constant anxiety. A new therapist replaced the last one I had seen, and I started getting more out of my weekly sessions. I hadn't told Kriss about my desire to change my gender, and it started to weigh on me. When I told her over Thanksgiving, I assumed it would be the end of our relationship, but instead, we grew together, learning what we could about how gender transition could happen. It triggered severe anxiety, but I knew if I didn't figure it out, it was likely to cause another catastrophic burnout. Through a friend, I learned about a gender clinic, and started working my way through their program.

At work, the shop owner decided to send me back to school as part of my job. It forced me to discuss my pending gender transition with him, as it wouldn't be fair to have him pay tuition only to turn around and fire me. I started my medical transition a month after classes started. My life was busy, but rewarding, and for the first time in my life, I was in surprisingly supportive relationships both at home and at work. By the time Kriss and I moved from Chicago to Oakland, I had avoided another burnout for over five years, knew better how to manage my anxiety, and had completed all but a couple of legal steps in my transition. For the first time, I left a major job on good terms, and while I didn't want to leave it, the change was mostly positive.

Our lives were radically changed by the move to Oakland. We arrived during the dotcom boom to work for a startup. It had been a remote gig, but the funders insisted everyone had to work in one office. We figured that it would be easier for me to re-employ than Kriss, as she started losing good jobs when her wheelchair became a full time need. The day before we moved, all remote tech support staff were fired except for Kriss, including me. While I was rehired three weeks after our arrival, the stress of the job losses and move triggered another, shorter burnout, and I stopped doing anything creative.

While I was glad for a break from weekly therapy sessions, I struggled with gender dysphoria, even though I was taking HRT and had had chest surgery. My sex drive also disappeared, and I was cranky and withdrawn. It was brutal in terms of work expectations, and there was not much time to do anything but work. We were forced to move and scrambled to buy a place. More job changes happened, and the dot com bust and 9/11 put a drag on the job market. Kriss's health began to fail in ways we didn't understand, but had to figure out. Realizing that I would not be able to continue working tech as it was too stressful and volatile, combined with getting Kriss desperately needed healthcare, meant major changes needed to happen, quickly.

We decided to redevelop our studio practices in art, music, and design as a business. Parts of our families were supportive, and we started doing gallery shows, performances, and queer community activism. While it was stressful and frustrating at times, returning to a creative path was more rewarding than any of the tech work had been. We traveled extensively for art shows, and went to lots of doctor appointments. Kriss had major surgery that took a year to recover from, and I went to grad school so I could teach for supplemental income and for community involvement. Then Kriss had a second major surgery while I was still in school.

When I graduated into the econopocalypse of 2008, it soon became apparent that we needed more income than we were able to bring in from our art. I took on contract work as a stopgap. Our finances collapsed under the weight of medical and school debt, and work was hard to find. We declared bankruptcy. The stress triggered another burnout, which complicated looking for work. It took almost four years post-graduation for me to find a part time teaching position teaching media design at a small digital arts private college.

At first, it seemed like a good fit for my skills. The school was known locally as a place for misfits, and probably a third of the students were neurodivergent. It was the first outside job since the diner that found my late night schedule advantageous, as afternoon classes often ended at midnight. The course director that supervised me did her best to keep the work manageable, but before I had finished mandatory training in my primary department, I was recruited to teach classes in another. In less than a year, I was working more than full time hours. Feeling responsible for my students, I took on more and more classes, while the school bled faculty when management fell apart after the school's founder died. When the IT department started to collapse, I ended up doing tech work that I didn't want in order to keep my classes running. When I went out on disability, I was working for three academic programs, in IT, and had barely won a fight to become a full time employee.

In the five year span I worked at the college, a close friend experienced a serious mental health and substance abuse crisis, and he moved into our back apartment because we did not want him homeless. My mother was diagnosed with an aggressive, terminal cancer, and our friend's instability upended a months-long plan to visit her. Kriss and I got our friend's parents to intervene, and he went into treatment in his childhood home. My mom died a few months later. Then my father was diagnosed with cancer. A month after his treatment was deemed cancer-free, he dropped dead. For me, it was devastating. We had formed a close adult relationship that hadn't existed when I was younger. All of my coping skills started to dissolve.

I started complaining that I didn't have a filter anymore instead of joking about it. One of the classrooms I worked in was hot and loud, a combination of bad HVAC and computer fans in overdrive as a result. My student's names became a blur that I couldn't recall. The work days stretched to ten hours in the classroom, with no way to keep up with preparation. It started to destroy my personal life, and Kriss implored me to quit.

In an effort to reduce the stress and anxiety of the situation, we looked for anything to help. I had been denied coverage for hysterectomy for over twenty years, on three different occasions, but the Affordable Care Act made the discriminatory plan exclusions that insurance companies held for transgender care illegal. It took months to clear my teaching schedule to have time for surgery and recovery, but my managers and my doctors worked to make it possible. It was denied anyway, triggering a terrible combination of neurodivergent burnout and PTSD that forced me out on disability while resolving both physical and mental health issues. I was not able to return to that job, and seven years later, am still recovering from the worst burnout I have ever experienced.

Recovering from this latest burnout has been different. Maybe it is because I am older and understand how earlier experience shaped me, and I now have the ability to see the damage that my younger self could not. Fleeting experiences that were common but not troublesome now linger when triggered. What used to be a short flare of intolerance to bright light and loud sounds now lasts months before my nervous system finally decides to relax. My brain stops processing symbolic information when overwhelmed, and makes reading difficult, and processing otherwise simple logic impossible. Smell and taste shift, making eating complex, and sometimes impossible. My body doesn't always recognize when I am hot or cold, or if I need to eat. But it is slowly getting better, even while requiring more self awareness.

Writing about this forced me to reconsider how many episodes of burnout I experienced, and it was more than I wanted to admit. Who wants to say their entire adult experience is marked by what most consider abject multiple failures? I realized how much of a difference it makes when you have supportive people around you, and how fleeting that can be. While I don't think I completely understand how to prevent another burnout, I do believe I know enough to keep another one from rolling in like a tsunami throug my life again. And I really hope so, because I don't know how I might survive one more.

OVERWHIPPED

Ellery Elizabeth

I was destined to be a hard worker. Given a name that literally translates to that effect when I was born by my Catholic parents, their beliefs dictate disciplined production in more ways than one. I took it to heart. My early childhood was full of extra credit assignments, staying late after school to help my teachers, and drawings that were used as the "class example." Until middle school, when they no longer were. Suddenly I was so sad, and the effort had left. I couldn't bring it back. I was no longer a hard worker, much to the dismay of my parents and teachers. Assignments were late. I spoke as little as possible and made-up excuses to leave and cry in the hallway. Nominative determinism be damned.

I have a new name now. It means trees, something I never have to worry about living up to. At work, though, I still go by my birth name. There, I push myself to meet tight deadlines, work extra hours, and be an example for other employees. Nominative determinism is back on, but at a cost. I've learned through my life that what are natural responses to stress for me are often considered unprofessional to others. Eloping and shutting down are things I have done in the past when the stakes are too high and the communication fails me. The reprimands have been harsh, and lately, the weeks have been more stressful.

I don't know what else to do, but to watch a charming group of home bakers compete for a plate.

Ask me to rate the different international series of *Bake Off* and I will, but just as Susan from Kent puts passion into her baking, I have for my unofficial rankings of the greatest comfort watch franchise of our time. Ireland is nostalgic with its gaggle of papists, but the format isn't enough to distract me from overdue paperwork. Canada puts out familiar bakes with a regional flair, but it's—dare I say—too comforting, and I realize that I could have phrased something better five hours ago. No, if you want to really escape the confines of social expectations and the wheels of capitalism then the original, *Great British Bake Off*, is the best bet.

I sit on the couch, secured with a blanket and wedged between pillows to my left and a dog on my right. I made it home without walking out of the room while being spoken to, although everything inside of me said, *run*. Out of view in the kitchen lies a sink full of dishes and empty cans left to soak days ago. Blue light from the laptop screen flashes across my face. "Oh no," I murmur aloud. "He overwhipped the souffle."

The dog looks unbothered; she doesn't understand the importance of stable egg whites. If the egg whites are whipped too little, the souffle will lack its trademark airiness as well as its rise; however, if the egg whites are overmixed—as is the case here—the mixture will be too runny. I do not understand why it's important for me to know these things, I'm not itching to make a souffle. Sometimes I wish I knew less things that I won't use and instead more practical things like, 1) how to regulate my emotions in a way that doesn't involve gentle music and flour, 2) how to do that quickly so that I can take care of those dishes, and 3) by 1 and 2 I mean how to self-regulate in a way that is acceptable to others for someone who is in their mid-thirties and works a 9-5 job forty hours a week.

I have thought of picking up a "real" hobby. I know people who have a stressful day at work and go home to pick up a paintbrush. Deadline missed, meet embroidered coffee cup cozy. A bad review from the boss stings worse after crocheting a hat. As much as I want this, it ultimately feels counterintuitive. I am overwhelmed by the need to be productive in my job, and choosing a hobby with yet more emphasis on a finished product and a fixed schedule seems to be the antithesis of relaxation. I would rather watch a grandfather from Glasgow bake a cake.

Just as one baker goes home every week, I must shut my laptop and go to bed after the show is over. The dog follows me, ready to wedge me into bed once again. Tomorrow I will try to keep a steady voice and a clearer head, but honestly, I'll be thinking about that souffle, and how if they had been at home and not under so much pressure, that baker would've whipped their souffle perfectly, or at least, well enough.

SURVIVAL AT MY CORE

Joe Biel

Years ago, after a writing conference in Portland, Cristina visited me at my office. She asked an innocuous sounding conversational prompt, "If you weren't a book publisher, what would you do?" But that simple question isn't answerable. In fact, it's one that I've dodged my entire life. When I was eight I told everyone that I would be a lawyer when I grew up because they lie all day long and that seemed like a professional skill I could figure out. But even that reaction was manufactured merely to avoid the question of career day.

The reality, which I dumped on Cristina without hesitation is "I do this so that I don't wake up drinking myself to death in the gutter." Caught a bit off guard by my honesty, she pushed through, "No, really, what would you do?" and again I reinforced "I've tried lots of things. I really liked teaching but this is the only sustainable thing that I'm really capable of doing that doesn't undermine my self-image and ability to get out of bed every day. I really need a job where the daily tasks move the needle towards the stated purposes and outcomes." She looked at me, processing. We weren't alone. Another voice within earshot intoned, "Then I hope that you are able to continue doing this." A different voice intoned, "If that happens, you can stay on my couch."

Today, I have something of a support system but for the first 40 years of my life, I had something more akin to an undermining system. I would build something and someone else would come through behind me and destroy it. That's okay. As I finish up my 27th year of this career, these experiences made me more hardened and resolved. Over time, you build a thicker skin and don't give up easily. My life has been difficult so I built up grit. I think of it like a protective coating on top of my skin so that when a stranger on Twitter attempts to stab me in the heart with abusive characterizations, I turn and walk away. But none of this can save me from periodic bouts of burnout.

And nothing could prepare any of us for March 2020. I returned home from the same writer's conference—this time in San Antonio—to news reports that the virus I caught months earlier was actually a global pandemic. Watching videos of myself filmed at the time, my cheeks were flushed, my eyes were sunken, and my usual scathing wit was being dragged ten feet behind my sagging skinsuit. The news reports indicated that only essential businesses would be allowed to remain open. I panicked. The most important part of my daily routine was biking to work, performing a dozen vital functions onsite, checking ten other key performance indicators, cleaning up various messes, and biking home. I remained glued to updates as "essential" was being defined as self-determining. My friend Jordan suggested that I could bike to work at 5 AM, like I do every day, and then if I wasn't allowed to go inside, I could simply turn around and bike home. I wasn't sure if this would actually release my stress valve but upon listening to *The Loudest Girl in the World*, I learned that many other autistic people managed changing routines... by refusing to change their routines!

Through gritted teeth and bated breath, before too long almost every business was decidedly "essential," probably due to lobbying from the business associations. So I kept biking to work at 5 AM on streets that were even more deserted than usual. I watched as the local Starbucks baristas stood like zombies, facing an empty dining room, in the midst of an abandoned cityscape. But the more that everything changed, the more that I maintained order by doing exactly the same thing.

The problem was, I didn't know how to stop or take a rest. Before long, I realized that I was going to work seven days per week, working ten hour days. I had decided that in addition to my regular full-time work, I would finish writing my new book, *How to be Accountable*. All of this was based on the assumption that the economy would come to a grinding halt and we'd have to shift budgets to prevent staff layoffs, but have newfound time to attend to the neglected tasks of the past five years.

I decided that I'd move everything out of storage and reorganize our warehouse to make it fit. I began biking ten boxes of books out of our storage unit every morning before dawn. When it was completely emptied, I began emptying out my basement at home.

Of course, the exact opposite happened. After a 47-day moratorium on budgets, reprints, and spending, orders were at an all-time high. Readers were hungry and couldn't get enough. It became abundantly clear that 2020 was going to be our busiest year of all time and we needed *more* staff. And after working 100-hour weeks without a day off for months, I started to snap.

Then it happened. My companion of eight years, my service dog Ruby, whose health had been flagging over the past year, became less inclined to get out of bed. I figured that she was just getting older and needed more rest. The doctor had created other tools for managing my glucose, so I'd let her stay in bed sometimes. But then she'd pull away when I'd pet her head. It became undeniable that she was in considerable pain. But I was distracted and put off bringing her to the doctor.

This perhaps epitomizes the failures of my own coping mechanisms. I dig my heels in so deep that I can't always see that what I'm doing has ceased to make sense. By the time that Ruby had testing done, the doctor concluded that a growth had been pushing on her glands for some time. The day that I was scheduled to bring her in, she passed away around 7 AM. I had left her at home while I ran to work that morning, which included unloading the new comic book about her from the printer.[4] Through tears, I tried to explain to the doctor that I needed to cancel her appointment. It took a few times for them to understand

4 *Do Not Pet: A Service Dog's Graphic Tale* (2020, Microcosm)

that I would not need to reschedule; that it was too late. I beat myself up about that one for the next year and would have done anything to keep her alive. Anything, that is, other than change my schedule or slow down enough to notice that she was in serious trouble. But the thing is, I did notice that. And I registered it. And I knew this was the end. I can't really explain it, but I had seen this coming in my subconscious mind and knew there was no escaping it. I had begun having dreams about it. And as the doctor explained it, there was likely nothing that we could have done about it regardless. Even when I brought her in to have some teeth extracted a year before, they said that I should have all teeth extracted that would cause her pain for the rest of her life. So I guess they knew too. Though I tried to insist that they were wrong because only I knew her like that.

Ruby and I shared a bond that I have never shared with a person. She taught me how to be a person in the world that isn't expecting or built for you. She was dependent on me just as I was dependent on her. And she reached her burnout about the same time that I reached mine. She was just a bit more forthcoming about admitting it. I still cry about her just about every week and visit her grave to talk to her as I always have. She knew more words than I even taught her, so I figure at this rate she's probably smarter than any living person by now. And she continues to have so much to teach me.

And I started to listen. I took weekends off and ended my weekday at 2 PM. It became easier to honor her legacy and everything that she's done for me. I went through solid periods of guilt that I had outlived her, when it seemed clear ten years ago that she would outlive me, and those were the plans that we made. Gradually, I realized that the best way to honor her was to do everything that I could to keep myself alive. Which means foreseeing and circumventing burnout before its crushing hand is forcing me. Maybe that's her voice in my head or maybe she finally taught me the skills of how to take care of myself.

A VISIT OF JUDGMENT

Brian

Even the doctor's routine Q&A is not designed for a schizophrenic person:

Do you feel depressed?

For sure!

Feelings of suicide?

Sometimes daily.

Do you feel like hurting yourself?

Not now, but yes.

How often?

It's a crap shoot.

Do you feel safe at home?

I don't feel safe anywhere many days and that is if I know where I am at!

My family doctor understands these answers to some degree, but not fully. She meets me where she can with empathy but lacks a depth of understanding about the complexities. Really, even trained psychologists/psychiatrists rarely understand all of the ways that schizo affects a person. So I don't expect much from a family physician. But this information gap can raise issues when asking for meds or the normal question routine during every visit. Fortunately, she trusts my judgment.

She also understands having to get my anti-psych meds from overseas because of the rates charged by the U.S. pharmaceutical industry, which have raised eyebrows even for the doctors writing the prescription.

Doctors make notes the best that they can while not understanding schizophrenia whatsoever. The nurses seem uncomfortable with my answers but have gotten used to them. I feel pity from them during these regular check-ins. Sorry that you're dealing with me but this is the health industry you got into and mental health is a shit show as mysterious as it is devastating.

One instance of being treated less than human came from a hospital visit when I was literally crapping myself bloody. I went to the ER and upon getting interviewed by the admittance nurse, I told her that I take Invega and explained it was an antipsychotic. She paused for a second which seemed weird. I was then taken to a room to be looked at. For as few patients as there were, this took a mysteriously long time.

I ended up having what is called a rotavirus. I defecated so much that I tore my abdominal wall and now have two hernias. I was given a *lot* of morphine and commented to my wife how quiet the entire ER wing was. I later found out that it was because they had taken me to the psych wing. They had assumed that nothing was wrong with my GI tract. My ass was bleeding and yet my mind was viewed as the problem. They heard I was taking Invega and moved me to a more "secure" area away from the "normal" population. I felt like one of those pictures of older times of the asylums with the "patients," stashed away from the public eye, like human refuse.

I felt betrayed, ostracized and stigmatized as potentially problematic, violent or out of control. The alienation that the disease already comes loaded with is only magnified and multiplied when treated like an "other" among the "regular" patients. I learned to distrust ERs when giving my medication list so they wouldn't treat me like a leper. This was how the medical system treats those with mental illness even though they take an oath not to harm. Is that only applied to certain standards of who the patient is and what they suffer from? MD can also stand for May Discriminate.

I AM IRON MAN

Graham

Oh fuck, I'm going to college. This is really happening. And my twin brother Geoff won't be there! Good, fuck that guy! He's Mr. "good at everything" even though I'm smarter than him, I'll no longer have to follow him with everything I do. This is gonna be brilliant.

Hold up, wait a sec. How the fuck do I meet people? I've never had to worry about that. Geoff just brought them to me and I chose the ones I wanted and made them my friends. I guess, I suppose, I'll just act like Geoff when I have to meet people. It can't be too hard. Let's give this a shot. [takes a sharp breath]

Haha, I'm good at this, college is fun and I have loads of friends! It's all about sarcasm and saying funny shit that's kind of mean! Simple, just like Geoff! Ha! I've got this down, and my friends love being around me because of the shit I say! Oops, she didn't like that, oh, now she's crying, she needs to just get over it, this is how I am, MY FRIENDS LOVE IT!!! Why do I feel so sick in my stomach? This is disgusting. I notice it less if I'm drunk. Guess I'll just drink more then.

Ouch! Fuck, I just had the shit kicked out of me. Those guys didn't like the mean stuff I said about them, even though it *was* hilarious!! I figured out all of their insecurities in seconds and made jokes out of it. My friends couldn't hold in their laughter. But now I'm banned from this bar and I'm pretty sure these guys are gonna beat me up whenever they see me. That feels kind of dangerous. I'm scared about making my jokes now, but MY FRIENDS LOVE IT! I can't stop. Urgh this feeling is nauseating, I guess I'll just drink more then.

I'm scared, constantly scared about saying the wrong thing. Most of the girls I know call me an asshole for *being me*, and there are a good number of guys that will beat me up if they see me. I feel sick inside. I don't even know how to describe it, fuck I don't even want to describe it. I don't even want to leave the house but that would be weird so I'll just drink six coffees before I leave. I drink so much coffee, MY FRIENDS LOVE IT, it's one of my things. Yeah, coffee is pretty great, if I drink enough of it I can push through the fear of interacting with everyone! Genius!

Done. Got my degree. Made it through college and my parents think I'm amazing. Well, that's not quite right. What they actually said was "It's amazing how well you did, and how many friends you made". They said "You stopped hiding behind Geoff and became your own person." Wow, they are finally proud of the way I show up. Fuck Geoff, this feels amazing. Now I have to get a job to keep them proud. I'm an engineer now, I guess, I'm going to be just like Iron Man. He was someone to be proud of, I love Iron Man!

How do I be like Iron Man? Let's see, I've already figured out the mean sarcasm piece, now I just need people to follow me like a leader. That means I have to make people do what I want, easy, I'll just figure out what type of person they like to work with, and I'LL BE THAT PERSON!

OMG this is so easy, after one meeting I pretty much know just how to BE THE PERSON THEY WANT and then they'll trust me. I'm so good at this that I keep getting promoted. They are giving me bigger and bigger jobs and I JUST *BECOME* THE PERSON I need to be for the job. Everyone is doing things so inefficiently, every place I go I meet people, I gain their trust, figure out what they do and then I make their work more efficient. I felt disgusting the other day after I changed some stuff and we fired half the team. But my boss was so impressed I GOT A *BIGGER* JOB. My parents are so proud of me. I got drunk that weekend and hooked up with someone. That disgusting feeling disappeared after that.

I've been traveling a lot now. I spend half my time in airplanes and hotels, to quote Iron Man... there is NOTHING BUT THE MISSION! In the last year I found ways to close three entire manufacturing facilities. Hundreds of people lost their jobs—people that trusted me. Urgh, there it is again, disgustingness just sitting in my stomach but I AM SO GOOD AT MY JOB. They gave me another job now. I'm in charge of our products for the Navy ballistic nuclear missiles, holy fuck I did it.. **I AM IRON MAN!**

I can't believe I did it, but the thing is..

I'M EXPECTED TO KEEP DOING THIS. I AM MEANT TO DO THIS ALL MY LIFE!!!!

[sharp exhale]

I CANT KEEP DOING THIS, I CANT, I CANT, I CANT, I CANT, I CANT, I CANT.

I HATE THIS. I HATE THIS. I HATE THIS. I HATE THIS. I HATE THIS. I HATE THIS.

DON'T MAKE ME DO IT. DON'T MAKE ME DO IT. DON'T MAKE ME DO IT.

ITS NOT FAIR. ITS NOT FAIR. ITS NOT FAIR. ITS NOT FAIR. ITS NOT FAIR.

I QUIT.

Remains.

What if we cast away,

The agreements from our prior days?

Of who we were, and what we said,

And the many ways in which we chose to play.

Like a flower gone to fruit,

Its blossom all but blown away.

Have faith, and trust,

The fruit that will remain.

CONCLUSION

Joe Biel

Today I'm in the Amtrak station in Chicago on my way home from a four week trip. Even with conference attendance perhaps forever reduced, the trade show for regional bookselling in St. Louis was overwhelming with its lights and hundreds of attendees and long hours. I suffered a migraine on day two, when I also had two speaking engagements. And in middle age, I'm not sure if it's a good thing or a bad thing that I've just learned to power through and do it anyway, deeply medicated and putting on my best face, avoiding the bright lights.

Because, really, that's what neurodivergent people do. We perform anyway or we drown. So doing it under duress isn't really that much different. It's just the earlier signs of burnout.

Fortunately, my next stop was Cleveland, my hometown of nearly twenty years. And I'd be there for ten days. And I'd have my own space for the duration of that time. It doesn't hurt that I'm also the boss, so people listen more than they disregard or plow over me.

It was interesting. I've only ever lived alone once before in my life, as I turned 30, living in a treehouse through the winter. It was liberating and powerful not to have to suffer the whims of others imposed on me. That freedom warmed me from the biting cold wind and the abusive relationship that I had narrowly escaped, and certainly not unscathed. But I wasn't yet comfortable in my skin then. I was, as one friend put it, "dragging my corpse behind me as I ran from dangers." And she wasn't wrong.

So this time in Cleveland, it was really the first time to both live alone for ten days *and* be comfortable in my skin. I felt like I was experiencing life in the 1950s. I'd prepare tea and breakfast in the morning and pack it all up before my carpool arrived to bring me to work. I'd work eight hours in the warehouse and then get dropped off to figure out dinner and watch television *on an actual television* before I fell asleep a few hours later. In the morning I'd wake up and do it all over again. In the sense of freeing routine and predictability, that week rebuilt me after being surrounded by a black hole, as I teetered on the edge of burnout for months. I'm glad that I got that experience and that it was only temporary because I do believe there's a danger to becoming too comfortable and complacent.

So I moved on to my next stop in Chicago. My friend who had lived mere blocks from the event I was attending had now moved eight miles north. So the commutes were about 20% of my waking hours. Then the event itself had been degraded from being in a downtown hotel to a maze-like warehouse with little signage and an incomprehensible layout. The concrete floors threatened to crush me from below as the fluorescent lights promised to melt me from above, but I had built up coping skills over the past weeks and years. I knew to stop and remove myself from the people periodically, to take breaks for snacks and meals, and to call it a day when I was fading. We could come back the next day and finish up. Even four-hour days under those conditions could feel very long. And before long, objectives were accomplished and it was time for everyone to pack up and go home.

The events were highly successful. I cannot understate the importance of that. Nothing feels worse than failure. Other than maybe burnout. But feeling like you accomplished your objectives is one of the greatest gifts to your self-image that you can offer, even the small things, like recognizing when you need a break or a meal. There are people that I like there and people that felt far too intense for me. Oh, and there was the guy from New Jersey who got six inches from my face and made demands of how we will conduct business before he said "hello," that were just short of threatening.

Fortunately, I'm experienced enough to know how to handle myself in these situations. A lot of it is simply not offering much in terms of emotional reciprocity, which comes naturally to me! So I'm heading home now, where I'm excited to see my chosen "family"[5] after so much time apart. Once again I have narrowly escaped the clutches of burnout.Hang in there! You can do it too!

5 One of them once quipped "Wow, you're like family to me!" to which I responded "I'm sorry. What did I do to hurt you so badly?" and then she said "Fair, I guess you're more like what family *should* be.

CONTRIBUTORS

Joe Biel is a self-made #ActuallyAutistic publisher and filmmaker who draws origins, inspiration, and methods from punk rock. Joe is the founder/manager of Microcosm Publishing and co-founder of the Portland Zine Symposium and author of twelve books, including *Good Trouble: Building a Successful Life & Business with Autism*. JoeBiel.net

Eliot Daughtry is the Director of Technological Arts and co-owner of killer banshee studios, a collaborative project lab dedicated to queer art, performance, music, and literature. An award winning artist in his own practices, he and partner Kriss De Jong have also recorded and produced artists including Deep Dickcollective and Tribe 8. eliot@killerbanshee.com

Kriss De Jong is the cover artist and is half of Killer Banshee Studios—the antidote to de-skilling. Eliot and Kriss have been living and creating together for over 25 years. We make queer: Art objects. Live video performance. Visual art. Music. Literature. Kriss is: Queer. Freak. Artist. Musician. Geek. Crip Cyborg. Intersexed. Neurodivergent. #ActuallyAutistic. kbanshee@killerbanshee.com

Partly Robot is the alter ego of Andrew Coltrin. Andrew stumbled onto his autism diagnosis after he stopped working in used bookstores and started working in schools. After burning out on being an English teacher, he's been an undercover angel working in the special ed programs of schools in Arizona and Oregon. He also writes odd things and periodically posts on his website PartlyRobot.com.

Amelia Nagoski, D.M.A. (it stands for Doctorate of Musical Arts), was an Associate Professor and Coordinator of Music at Western New England University. Her job is to run around waving her arms and making funny noises and generally doing whatever it takes to help singers get in touch with their internal experience.

"Brian" anonymously lives and works in Ohio and may be contacted through this zine.

Graham Hulbert is #madebydyslexia. He is an engineer, a maker, and a change leader. In his job he helps companies build sustainable practices and strategies that allow them to revel in a changing environment. Outside of work he can be found either in his workshop fixing old things/making new things, or in the mountains writing poetry and volunteering for the forest service. You can find him on Instagram at @ iaminstagwam.

Ellery Elizabeth is not her real name.

SUBMIT

If you're neurodiverse or an ally, you can submit to the next issue of ***Neurodivergent Pride***, which has the theme of ***Animal Companions.*** The deadline is ***March 1, 2023***. The following issue's theme is ***Mutual Aid*** and the deadline is ***July 1, 2023.*** Submissions should be 500-2,000 words or art.

If ***you are neurodivergent,*** you should submit ***500-2,000 words*** exploring any aspect of the theme.